Cambridge College Walks

F.A. REEVE

THE OLEANDER PRESS OF CAMBRIDGE

The Oleander Press
17 Stansgate Avenue
Cambridge CB2 2QZ

ISBN 0 900891 42 4

Reeve, Frank Albert
   Cambridge college walks –(Cambridge town,
   gown and county; vol.25).
   1. University of Cambridge – Description –
   Guide Books
   I. Title II. Series
   914.26'59   LF127

Designed by Ron Jones

Printed and bound by Burlington Press, Foxton

Introduction

Cambridge has a population of about 100,000 and is the main shopping and regional centre for about 400,000 people. Planning policies have sought to exclude large-scale industries, and many houses have been built in adjacent villages in order to avoid a rapid increase in the population of the city. It is pre-eminently a university city. Although there were students at Oxford about twenty years earlier than at Cambridge, the latter is a much older city.

There was an unfortified Belgic settlement on the high ground at Castle Hill, and the Romans eventually had an enclosure of about 28 acres. Cambridge became important in very early times because it was the only place where people travelling between East Anglia and the rest of England could cross the river. To the north, the undrained Fenlands were impassable, and to the west and south there were dense forests. By the tenth century, merchants traded in many commodities brought up the river from King's Lynn. After the Norman Conquest, King William built a castle which was improved and enlarged by later kings, but by the reign of Queen Elizabeth it had fallen into disrepair.

Barnwell Priory, established in 1112 on the outskirts of the town, was one of the largest in England, with a church 200 feet long, and the nunnery of St. Radegund in Jesus Lane also had a magnificent church. Franciscan friars arrived in 1225 and later built a monastery in Sidney Street; the Dominicans were building on the site now occupied by Emmanuel College by 1238; and many other religious orders settled in the town.

The date when the first students arrived in Cambridge is uncertain, but we do know that in 1209 an Oxford woman was killed, allegedly by a student. The mayor seized some of his friends as hostages, and King John gave him leave to hang them. Many frightened students fled from Oxford, and some came to Cambridge. At first they lived in inns or private houses, later in houses for students known as hostels. The medieval students were usually only fourteen or fifteen years old, they were high-spirited and ill-disciplined, and there were constant affrays with the townspeople.

The students complained that they were overcharged for

rents and food, and four officials called Taxors, two Masters, and two townsmen, were appointed to supervise the market and assess rents. There were serious riots in 1261 when sixteen townsmen were executed, and again in 1381 when university and college property was attacked and university records were burned in the Market Place.

The Masters lectured in hired houses and the university did not erect any buildings for teaching for the first 200 years of its existence. The head of the university was the Chancellor, who had his own court which could try all cases involving students, whom he could imprison, expel or excommunicate.

The first college was founded in 1284 and seven others in the first half of the fourteenth century. Colleges were founded and endowed to provide accommodation and a small stipend for poor scholars who were teaching in the university, and did not at first admit students. All of the early colleges were very small, with only a dining-hall, kitchen and chambers, and some commenced in existing houses and only later began to erect their own buildings.

No good building stone is to be found near Cambridge, and many of the early buildings were constructed of clunch, a hard chalk quarried locally. By the eighteenth century, some of the colleges were in a bad state of repair, and the walls were faced with stone.

By the sixteenth century, Sturbridge Fair, held annually for five weeks just outside the town, had become the largest in England. Merchants came from all parts of the British

4

Plan of Cambridge ▷

1 Fitzwilliam College	8 Trinity College	15 Emmanuel College	22 Downing College
2 New Hall	9 Christ's College	16 St Catharine's College	23 Newnham College
3 Churchill College	10 Caius College	17 Corpus Christi College	24 Darwin College
4 Magdalene College	11 Trinity Hall	18 Queens' College	25 The Fitzwilliam Museum
5 St John's College	12 The Old Schools and the Senate House	19 Pembroke College	26 The Chemical Laboratory
6 Jesus College	13 Clare College	20 Selwyn College	27 University Library
7 Sidney Sussex College	14 King's College	21 Peterhouse	

Isles and from abroad. Many Cambridge scholars were influenced by the doctrines of Martin Luther, and laid the foundations of the Reformation. Cambridge played an important role in national affairs during the Civil War, when Oliver Cromwell made the town the headquarters of the Eastern Counties Association, and it was the military and administrative centre for the whole of East Anglia.

From the sixteenth century onwards, when more colleges had been founded or enlarged, most of the teaching took place within each college, but this system broke down by the middle of the nineteenth century, because more subjects were being studied and most colleges could not provide adequate instruction. Men who took their studies seriously had to go to private tutors. Though some of the colleges were rich, the university itself had only a small income and could not finance the building of lecture-rooms and the laboratories which the development of science had made necessary.

This unsatisfactory state of affairs was considered by several Royal Commissions, and revised statutes came into force in 1882. Henceforth, colleges had to contribute to university funds. The university now receives annual grants from the Government, and organizes the lectures and the examinations. The colleges are independent corporations which derive their income from the past benefactions and the fees paid by students.

A college elects its **Fellows**, i.e. senior members, most of whom have teaching posts in the university, though some have administrative duties within their college. Today, more than a thousand persons are engaged in teaching or research, and hundreds of other people are employed on primarily administrative duties in libraries, museums, scientific laboratories, and similar institutions.

Each college selects its students, and only members of the colleges may study in the university. Formerly, most of them came from the great public schools, but this is no longer so, and most receive state grants. Within the colleges **Tutors** and **Directors of Studies** supervise the academic work of the students, and allocate them to a **Supervisor**, who may not be a member of the same college. The student pays a weekly visit to his supervisor to be given advice about his studies, and often prepares an essay which is discussed with the supervisor. This system is very important because it provides an intimate relationship between a student and a teacher.

There are about 10,000 undergraduates, about one-fifth of whom are women. The first college for women was not founded until 1869 and, although in 1881 women were allowed to take the tripos examinations, successful candidates were not given degrees until 1947. There are thirty colleges, only three of them for women, but recently some of the men's colleges have begun to admit a few women.

The academic year begins in October, and there are three terms, each eight weeks. Most of the students stay for three years, but about 10% remain longer for more advanced study or research. There are over 2,000 graduates, some of whom come from other British or foreign universities to do research or to gain a higher degree.

Undergraduates are accommodated within a college for at least some of their time at the university, and for the remainder of the time in lodgings, or in a hostel or house belonging to the college and situated elsewhere in the city. Most of the lectures are given in the mornings, and some of the undergraduates devote the afternoons to sport. Colleges have their own playing-fields and boathouses, sometimes shared with another college.

Men who represent the university in a sporting encounter with Oxford are called **blues**, light blue for Cambridge and dark blue for Oxford. The most important blues are those who take part in the annual boat race on the Thames or in the rugby match played at Twickenham.

There are hundreds of societies and clubs which cater for a bewildering variety of interests. At the beginning of October, each of these university and college organisations has a small stand in the Societies Fair at the Corn Exchange and seeks to enrol new members.

A student may find that a world-famous scholar has rooms on the same staircase. Nobel Prizes are awarded annually by the Swedish Academy of Sciences to those who have contributed most to the common good in the domains of physics, chemistry, physiology or medicine. Up to 1977, forty-six of the prizes have been won by Cambridge men: twenty-one for physics, eleven for chemistry, and fourteen for physiology or medicine. Cambridge is the home of more Nobel Prizewinners than any other place and, over the years, Trinity College alone has provided seventeen of them.

The city itself possesses few outstanding buildings apart from the churches, though King's Parade, Trinity Street and St. John's Street are among the most attractive streets in England. The only large recent commercial development is in Lion Yard, a pedestrian precinct, which includes a splendid new public library.

The grounds of the colleges beside the river are supplemented by several attractive commons belonging to the city; in fact few other towns of a comparable size have so many open spaces. Many visitors enjoy a trip on the river. Boats may be hired at the bottom of Mill Lane for the river towards Grantchester, also from here and from near Magdalene Bridge for the section passing through college grounds.

First Walk

Queens' — King's - Clare — Trinity Hall — Trinity — St. John's

This begins at Silver Street Bridge, from which there are interesting views on both sides. On one side is the Mill Pool which, until the coming of the railway, was often completely filled with barges which brought many different commodities. On the far side of the Pool there were two corn mills from very early times until 1928, when the buildings then existing were demolished. The large building to the left was formerly a granary and later a boat-building works.

From the other side of the bridge one can see the curious wooden bridge of Queens' College, which was built in 1902 and is a copy of a similar bridge designed by W. Etheridge and constructed in 1749-50. The beams of the original bridge were fitted together without any nails or bolts.

Queens' College was founded in 1446 by Andrew Dockett, Rector of the nearby church of St. Botolph, as the College of St. Bernard, for a President and four Fellows. Two years later he was aided by Margaret of Anjou, queen of Henry VI, who asked her husband to allow her to refound and rename the college because, as she said, "in the whiche Vniuersite is no college founded by eny Quene of England hidertoward". When Edward IV became king, further endowments were made by his queen Elizabeth Woodville, and the plural spelling Queens' commemorates the two royal ladies associated with the college.

To the left, just inside the entrance gate, is a new block of rooms and a dining hall. The grove beside the river is resplendent with daffodils in the Spring and, if you walk a little way along the path, there is an attractive view of the 16th-century Gallery of the President's Lodge. The building across the river near Silver Street Bridge was designed by Essex in 1756 to replace a range of 1564. At the time, the college intended to pull down all of the picturesque red-brick buildings beside the river and to extend Essex's building, but fortunately they were spared.

Cross the bridge and enter Cloister Court. Queens' was the first college to introduce cloisters. To the left is the attractive Gallery of the President's Lodge, constructed of timber and plaster, some of the materials coming from a Carmelite Priory formerly on part of the site of the college.

Until 1911 the timber framing was covered with plaster. A gallery of this type was often called an 'ambulatorium magistri' in early records, and was intended as a place where the Master could take exercise in bad weather.

The famous European scholar Erasmus came to Cambridge in 1510 and for several years lived in Queens' College. According to tradition, he occupied rooms at the top of the turret on the right. He was the first man to teach Greek in the university, and no doubt worked on his important critical edition of the New Testament in that language.

Go through the doorway on the right side of the court, passing the Hall on the left. Unfortunately it is normally closed to the public, although it can sometimes be viewed from the passage. A striking feature is the rich coloured decorations of the restored mid-15th-century roof. The original fireplace was improved in 1861 with tiles designed by William Morris and Ford Madox Brown, and Bodley designed the decorations above it.

The Principal Court was begun in 1448 and quickly completed; it is the earliest Cambridge quadrangle of real architectural merit. The red bricks used were probably imported from Holland and were so durable that the court remains practically as it was built. To the left is the Library, and beyond it the former Chapel licensed for services in 1454 and now used as a reading room. The picturesque sundial on the wall, which is also a moondial, was put up in 1642 and restored in 1733.

The entrance Gateway flanked by towers was the third large gateway to be built in Cambridge. Similar gateways are a conspicuous feature of several of the colleges. Go through a passage on the left side of the court into Walnut Tree Court. The range to the right, in Tudor style, was built in 1617 and partly rebuilt in 1778 after a fire.

The new Chapel, designed by Bodley in 1891, has a lofty and colourful interior. The modern Erasmus Building designed by Sir Basil Spence, architect of the new Coventry Cathedral, was erected in 1960, and most of the ground floor has been left open to preserve a view of the Backs (the Cambridge name for the grounds of the colleges on the west side of the river). There was much controversy when the plans for this building were published, since Queens' retains more of its medieval buildings than any other college, and many people opposed the erection of a modern block so close to them.

Leave the college by the gate into Queens' Lane and turn left. This narrow street was originally called Milne Street and was one of the most important in the medieval town, running from Silver Street and across the present site of King's College to Trinity College.

Ahead is a gateway into **King's College**. In 1441, Henry VI had already founded Eton College in Berkshire and wished to build a college in which his Eton scholars

◁ Queens' College

could continue their studies. His first plan was for a small college of about twelve scholars, and he acquired a site behind the Old Schools north of the present Chapel. Soon after building began, he decided to enlarge his scheme to accommodate 70 scholars, 10 priests, 16 choirboys and 6 clerks, for which he needed a much larger area. The ground was an important part of the medieval town, with lanes leading from the High Street and Milne Street to riverside wharves. The church of St Zachary, a small college named Godshouse, and houses, were all demolished, and the king made detailed plans for a magnificent court, a Chapel on one side, a 3-storey range with an imposing gateway towards the street, and other ranges to contain the Hall and the Library. A further court would have a kitchen, bakehouse and brewery, and to the west of the Chapel there would be a cloistered cemetery and a very lofty bell-tower.

The only part of this grandiose scheme to be carried out was the Chapel, and most of the site remained empty for about 300 years. The construction of the Chapel began in 1446, in a white magnesium limestone from Yorkshire, and by 1462 the walls were probably about 60-70 feet high at the east end, but only 7-8 feet towards the west. Work then almost ceased for about fifteen years, and was resumed in 1476. When the five easternmost bays had been completed, they probably had a temporary roof. Henry VII came to Cambridge in 1506 and decided to complete the building. About 140 workmen were employed, using an oolitic limestone from the Clipsham and Peterborough districts and from Weldon. John Wastell, the master mason of the period 1508-15, who had worked at Canterbury, constructed the great vault, the corner turrets, the pinnacles on the buttresses and the porches. It had taken about seventy years to complete the exterior.

The Chapel is normally open: during terms, weekdays 9.00 — 15.45, Sundays 14.00 — 15.00 and after the service until 17.45. During vacations, weekdays from October to April, 9.00 — 17.00; from May to September, 9.00 —17.45. On Sundays, 10.30 — 17.00. During terms there are choral services on weekdays, except Mondays, at 17.30, and on Sundays at 10.30 and 15.30. The Chapel is sometimes closed for choir practices or recording.

King's College Chapel is one of the last English Gothic structures in the high Perpendicular style. It is very long and lofty, with little solid wall, as the twenty-six windows occupy most of the space. The delicate fan-vaulting of the roof, a style not found in any other country, and probably the most beautiful form of roofing ever invented, is one of the supreme achievements of English architects. The total length of the stone ribs is about two miles. Henry VI had stipulated that the interior walls should be plain and without much ornamentation, but the walls of the ante-chapel have numerous finely-carved stone coats of arms, supported by dragons and greyhounds, also crowns, roses and portcullises, all symbols of the Tudor kings.

Eighteen side-chapels were formed by roofing over the

King's College Chapel

spaces between the buttresses, and in one of these, to the right, is the tomb of John Churchill, the only son of the first Duke of Marlborough, who died of smallpox while he was a student at King's.

The large west window depicting the Last Judgement was completed in 1879, but the glass in all of the other windows was put in between 1515 and 1531. It is the largest and best preserved amount of ancient coloured glass anywhere in the world. York Minster is the only other great medieval church in England to possess its original glass. Most of the subjects in the lower parts of the windows are from the New Testament, and those in the upper parts are scenes from the Old Testament that mostly correspond with the subjects beneath. The large east window depicts the Crucifixion. The total area of the glass, which was removed for safety during the Second World War, is about 1,200 square yards.

During the reign of Henry VIII the choir was paved with marble, a high altar set up, and the screen and the stalls constructed. The screen is the earliest large timber structure in the country completely in the Renaissance style. It was executed by foreign craftsmen, probably Italian, and it is claimed that it is the most magnificent wood carving of its period to be found anywhere north of the Alps. It was constructed between 1513 and 1536, that is between the marriage of Anne Boleyn to Henry VIII and her execution, and above the doorway one can see the initials H and A. The doors of the screen, with the arms of Charles I, were

11

provided in 1636. Thomas Dallam built an organ in 1606 and the present instrument of 1688 has been reconstructed and enlarged several times. The angels with the trumpets were set up in 1859.

The lectern, surmounted by a small statue of Henry VI, was presented by Robert Hacomblen, Provost at the beginning of the 16th century. The stalls were made by the workers who executed the screen. The armorial panelling was added in 1633 and shows the arms of the universities of Oxford and Cambridge, the colleges of Eton and King's, and the English kings from Henry VI to Charles I. The canopies were added by Cornelius Austin, a Cambridge joiner, in 1675-8.

In 1961, Mr. Alfred Alnatt bought Rubens's painting, *The Adoration of the Magi,* for £275,000, and presented it to the college. It was painted on wood in 1634 as the altar piece for a convent in Louvain. Before it could be placed beneath the east window, the floor had to be lowered and the high altar and some Victorian panelling removed: there is now a simple altar with a cloth designed by Joyce Conway Evans, with gold thread and pearls from Japan. The Chapel was restored and cleaned internally in 1965-8 at a cost of over £150,000. Underfloor heating was installed, and the paving renewed with 1,000 black marble slabs from Belgium and 850 white slabs from Italy.

The Fellows' Building, at right angles to the Chapel, was designed by Gibbs and completed in 1730. Two other ranges to complete the court were projected, but not built.

In white Portland stone, it is one of the architect's best works, and the style is very classical for its period. No further building then took place for almost a century. William Wilkins won a competition in 1823 and erected the Hall and other buildings on the south side of the court, also the screen and gatehouse towards King's Parade. Wilkins proposed to 'Gothicise' Gibbs' Building, but fortunately lack of funds prevented this.

The Fountain was set up in 1879. When it was planned, the Provost was concerned about how a supply of water could be obtained for it, and William Whewell, Master of Trinity, suggested that they should build a waterworks. They proceeded to form a Waterworks Company to the great benefit of the town and the university.

It is worth while to walk to the bridge of 1818 to see one of the finest views in Cambridge. Beyond a wide expanse of lawn laid down in the middle of the 18th century rise the Fellows' Building and the Chapel, and the south side of Clare College. One can also see Clare Bridge, the oldest and the most beautiful of the college bridges.

Until 1892, this part of the river was the scene of an interesting annual ceremony, the Boat Procession, which took place on the day after the concluding day of the May Races. About thirty college eights, decorated with flags and flowers, assembled in the Mill Pool, and were then ranged across the river between the bridges of King's and Clare. The head of the river crew remained seated while the other crews stood with uplifted oars and drank a toast to them,

King's College, with Clare to the left

then each crew was toasted in turn. Crowds of about ten thousand persons watched these ceremonies. Strings of barges which brought goods to Cambridge were mostly pulled by horses walking on the towpath. When the colleges laid out their grounds beside the river, the towpaths were abolished, the bed of the river was gravelled, and the horses then walked in the river.

Leave King's College by the gate to the north of the Chapel. The buildings on the right occupy the site of the old court of King's which was sold to the university in 1829. They were reconstructed in 1864-7 and now house the Registry and other university offices. The ornate gateway had remained unfinished until it was completed by J.L. Pearson in 1890. Through the gateway one can see one of the ancient buildings forming the Old Schools, the first buildings erected by the university for teaching.

The roadway here was originally a part of Milne Street and to the left is **Clare College**. In 1326 the university obtained a royal licence to settle scholars in two houses, and twelve years later the college was refounded by Lady Elizabeth de Clare, a granddaughter of Edward I. Just before the Civil War, the college was in such a bad state of repair that it was necessary to rebuild. The frontage of the old court was near the road, and Clare proposed to set back the new buildings to give more light and air to themselves and to King's, and a better view of King's Chapel. In recompense, Clare sought to have a passage through a field across the river, then belonging to King's. After a long controversy, Clare was able to lease this ground and built their bridge in 1639-40. The east and south ranges of the court were finished by 1642, then the Civil War caused work to be suspended until 1669. Cromwell seized materials to fortify the Castle. Seventy-seven years elapsed before the court was complete, but architectural unity was maintained, and when it was finished some people said that it looked more like a palace than a college.

Enter the court and turn to the right to visit the Chapel designed by James Burrough and continued after his death by James Essex. It was built in 1763-9, and has an octagonal antechapel with a glazed lantern, an elliptical barrel-vaulted plaster ceiling and an elliptical east end with a semi-dome. The painting is by Giovanni Cipriani Battista (1727-1785?), the artist who executed the panels on the Coronation Coach. The Hall was begun in 1683 and was remodelled internally in 1870, when the fine plaster ceiling was constructed. The plain wall panelling is original. The influence of Wren's chapel at Emmanuel College caused the design of the river front of the court to be drastically altered, and the master mason, Robert Grumbold, introduced giant pilasters. The bridge, with three spans of nearly semicircular arches, has parapets surmounted by stone balls. To the right, beyond the bridge, is the Fellows' Garden, one of the most beautiful in Cambridge, and normally open in the afternoons from Mondays to Fridays.

Leave Clare by the gate at the end of the avenue and turn to the right, then right again into Garret Hostel Lane.

Clare College quadrangle

This was given to the town by Henry VI after his acquisition of the site for his college had closed other lanes leading to the river. The fine modern bridge was a gift to the city from Sir Harry Trusted and his two sons, former students of Trinity Hall. From both sides of the bridge there are beautiful views of the river and of the bridges of Trinity and Clare.

Enter **Trinity Hall**, a college with a long legal tradition, by a 15th-century gateway which formerly stood at the front of the college. Trinity Hall, first called the College of the Scholars of the Holy Trinity of Norwich, was founded in 1350 by Bishop Bateman to train more lawyers for the Church and State after the ravages of the Black Death.

On the left is the charming little 16th-century Library built of brick, with a large stepped gable and Gothic windows. The curious small door on the upper floor was no doubt formerly reached by an external wooden staircase. The library retains its original bookcases and benches, and is usually open from 10.30 to 12.30 during term.

The Hall was reconstructed in 1743-5 and enlarged in 1892. The Front Court, at the end of the 14th century, was the largest then existing. The east range was rebuilt by Salvin in 1852 after it had been destroyed by fire. The other sides were ashlar-faced in 1730-45 and the windows were enlarged, but in the northwest corner one of the original small windows is still visible. The very small Chapel was built by 1366 and slightly extended in 1864. The most striking feature is the fine plaster ceiling of 1730 with

Trinity College Great Gate

richly-coloured shields of arms and large sunflowers.

Leave Trinity Hall and turn to the left, then to the right into Trinity Lane. On the left is the rear of the south range of the Great Court of Trinity, and the tall chimneys make an interesting view. Turn left into Trinity Street and note the picturesque Elizabethan building on the right, now the Turk's Head Restaurant, but formerly one of the many coffee-houses frequented by students in the 17th and 18th centuries. It later housed Foster's, the second bank to be established in Cambridge, the first being Mortlock's.

Trinity College was founded in 1546 by Henry VIII, and is the largest in the university. The king amalgamated two existing colleges, Michaelhouse founded in 1323, and King's Hall founded in 1336, with some hostels, and gave his college large revenues, derived chiefly from suppressed religious houses, and special privileges.

The Great Gate was completed by 1535 and bears the coats of arms of Edward III and his six sons. The third shield from the left is that of the Black Prince; the shield of William of Hatfield is blank because he died young before he had been granted arms. The statue represents Henry VIII, and in his right hand he should be holding a sceptre, but someone removed it and replaced it by a wooden chairleg. Somewhat incongruously too, the king is wearing a flimsy crown above a hat. In the 18th century an observatory was built on the top of the gate. An interesting ceremony takes place here when a new Master arrives for the first time to take up his appointment. The gates are closed, and he has to knock and present his credentials before he is admitted. The statues on the court side of the Great Gate depict James I flanked by his queen, Anne of Denmark, and his son Charles. The statue of the king has weathered badly, as it was carved from a block of clunch, a hard chalk quarried locally, and it has been given a new head.

Great Court, the largest court in either Oxford or Cambridge, was created by Dr. Thomas Nevile, Master 1593-1615. A rich man and a favourite of Queen Elizabeth, he completed ranges of chambers on the east and south sides, then demolished a part of King's Hall which projected into the court. He extended the Master's Lodge and built a Library towards the Chapel. The Gate of King Edward III, which originally stood where there is now a sundial, was taken down and rebuilt between the Library and the Chapel. The large ornamental fountain was begun in 1602. The water for it comes from an underground conduit constructed in 1325 by the Franciscans to bring water from a spring 1,800 yards away. It is now supplemented by an artesian well.

On entering the court, you should first turn to the right. Thackeray occupied the ground-floor rooms adjoining the Gate, Macaulay those next to the Chapel, and Sir Isaac Newton those above. The Chapel, in the Gothic style, was erected in 1555-67 and, in the first year of its construction, nearly 3,000 loads of stone came from the dissolved Franciscan Friary.

In the antechapel there are statues of Bacon, Barrow,

Macaulay, Whewell and Tennyson, all seated, and a standing figure of Newton, a masterpiece of sculpture by Louis-François Roubiliac (1755). Tennyson was fond of smoking, so the donor of the statue arranged with the sculptor that the poet's pipe should be shown near the base. The magnificent screen with Corinthian columns between the antechapel and the chapel, like the stalls and baldacchino, were erected during the mastership of Richard Bentley (1700-42). The windows acquired their stained glass in the 19th century.

King Edward's Tower (1428-32) was the first monumental gateway erected in Cambridge, and is the oldest building in the court. The statue of Edward III was put up in 1601, while the timber bell-turret is modern, but a copy of the original. The large and magnificent Master's Lodge in the northwest corner of the court was improved by Bentley. Newton was knighted in the drawing-room by Queen Anne.

The Hall, also built at the expense of Nevile in 1604-8, is the largest college hall in Cambridge and is a copy of that in the Middle Temple. It is normally open to the public on weekdays, 10.00-12.00. There are large oriels on both sides of the dais, containing a great deal of heraldic glass, and numerous portraits of former Masters and scholars, including a full-length, life-size portrait of Henry VIII by Eworth, derived from a Holbein portrait. From 1702 until 1866 the Hall was heated by a large iron dish standing on legs and burning charcoal.

The steps leading towards the Hall from Great Court present a challenge to athletes, and the father of Lord Montgomery is said to have been the first to scale them in one jump. On the far side of the Screens you will emerge on to a Tribune built in 1682. Nevile's Court was built in an Italianate style and finished in 1612, although it was then only about three-fifths of its present length, and was closed by a wall with a large central gate which was re-erected later as the entrance to the college in Trinity Lane. The cloisters are original, but the fronts of the north and south ranges were rebuilt by Essex in 1755. During the first few months of the 1914-18 war, beds were placed in the cloisters for soldiers wounded in France and Belgium, and there were also marquees on the lawns.

Sir Christopher Wren's Library, begun in 1676, forms the far side of the court. Wren first suggested a circular domed building, but the plan adopted was for a 150ft.-long rectangular building: it is one of Wren's masterpieces. The statues on the roof represent Divinity, Law, Physics and Mathematics. Professor Pryme, who was at Trinity from 1799 until 1803, said that twenty years earlier, when the dons wore wigs, some students bribed the college barber, and borrowed dons' wigs, placing them during the night on the heads of the statues.

A staircase in the far corner to the right leads to the interior of the Library, which is open to visitors from

Trinity College Great Court ▷

Mondays to Fridays, from 2.15-4.45pm. and in term on Saturdays from 10.30-12.30. It is more spacious than one would imagine from the exterior. Wren designed the bookcases to run along the walls and also at right angles to them, to form thirty cubicles, and said that this arrangement "must needes prove very convenient and gracefull, and the best way for the students will be to have a little square table in each Celle with two Chaires". The ends of the bookcases and some of the walls are adorned with exquisite carvings in limewood made by Grinling Gibbons. There are marble busts, some by L.F. Roubiliac (1702-1762), and Bertel Thorvaldsen's statue of Byron which was intended for Westminster Abbey, but was not accepted, and remained in the Customs House for about twelve years until it was given to the college. The stained-glass window, designed by Cipriani and put up in 1774, depicts Fame introducing Bacon and Newton to George III. Some of the treasures of the Library are to be seen in showcases, among them a page from the Gutenberg Bible, the first book to be printed from movable type; a First Folio of the works of Shakespeare; manuscripts of John Milton; a copy of Newton's *Principia* annotated by the author, and a small notebook in which Newton recorded his expenses. There are also manuscripts by many other notable people connected with Trinity.

Leave the Library and walk beneath it to New Court, built in 1823-5 by Wilkins. Prince Charles had rooms in this court while he was an undergraduate. Go through the gateway to the right to the bridge built by Essex in 1763-65 and, after crossing the bridge, turn to the right and go over the small iron bridge to enter the grounds of St. John's College. The grounds of Trinity to the west of the river were laid out with gravelled walks and trees, during the mastership of Bentley, on low ground liable to flooding, and the level in both colleges has been artificially raised.

St. John's College is on the site of the Hospital of St. John founded in 1135 by Henry Frost, a rich burgess, to be conducted by a community of Augustinian canons who would care for poor and infirm townsfolk. John Fisher persuaded Lady Margaret Beaufort, the mother of Henry VII, to convert the Hospital into a college, but she died before she had made this provision in her will, and Fisher had to overcome many difficulties before the college opened in 1516.

On the far side of the lawn is New Court, built in a neo-Gothic style in 1825-31, when it was the largest single building in any college. The high central section of the building, with its four turrets and glazed lantern, is often called 'the wedding cake'. Go through New Court to see the modern Cripps' Building behind it, one of the best examples of modern architecture in Cambridge. It was designed by Powell and Moya to form two 3-sided courts accommodating about 200 students, and has a large punt lake near the river. Turn to the left to see the School of Pythagoras, the oldest secular building in the city, a Norman stone house once a farmhouse and the residence of

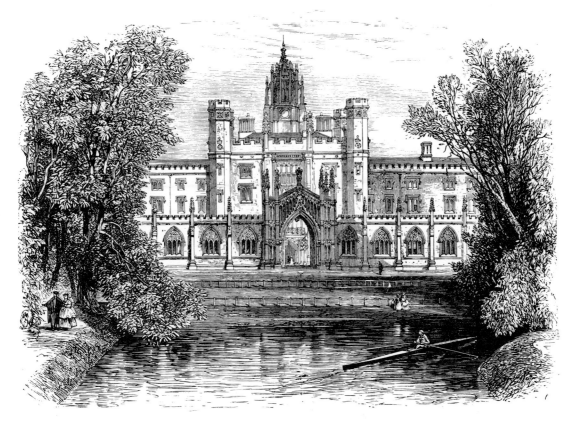

St. John's College, New Court

the first mayor of Cambridge. The origin of the curious name of the building remains a mystery. Return to the bridge built by Robert Grumbold in 1709-12 to designs based on suggestions made by Wren. Near the bridge is an ancient mounting-block. In former times the colleges kept many horses, not only for recreation, but because the estates owned by the colleges in many parts of the country had to be visited periodically. From the bridge we see the covered bridge, constructed to connect New Court with the older buildings, which was built in 1831 to the designs of Henry Hutchinson and is called the Bridge of Sighs, though it bears only a slight resemblance to its namesake in Venice. Some years ago, undergraduates brought a car up the river on four punts during the night, and suspended it beneath the bridge.

Beyond the Bridge of Sighs is the Library; the initials I.L.C.S. on the gable overlooking the river stand for Johannes Lincolniensis, Custos Sigilli, and refer to John Williams, Bishop of Lincoln and Lord Keeper of the Privy Seal, who was a former Fellow of St. John's and contributed two-thirds of the cost.

A small passage to the left leads into Third Court, and the Library, built in 1623-4, is on the far side. The tall two-light windows are a very early example of the Gothic Revival. Go through the large gatehouse into Second Court,

built in 1598-1602 with money given by the Countess of Shrewsbury. Her statue is above the arch. This court is an attractive example of Tudor architecture. The Master's Gallery once occupied the whole of the first floor to the left. About 45 feet at the west end were partitioned off to make a staircase to the Library, and in 1863-5 the main part, 93 feet long, became a Combination Room (Senior Fellows' Common Room). It is one of the finest rooms of its type in England, and during the Second World War, Eisenhower, Montgomery and others met there to discuss the plans for the landing in France.

The Hall is not open to the public. It is one of the finest in Cambridge, with a splendid hammerbeam roof. The portraits include Bishop Fisher and William Wordsworth, who described his rooms in *The Prelude*:

> Right underneath the college kitchens made
> a humming sound, less tuneable than bees,
> But hardly less industrious.

His rooms were incorporated into the kitchen in 1893.

First Court was built between 1511 and 1520, but was rendered less attractive when the south range was altered and ashlar-faced by Essex in 1772-5; the old chapel was demolished when the new large Chapel designed by Sir G.G. Scott was built in 1864-9. Stone kerbs indicate the position of the former building. The Hall was lengthened by 40 feet in 1862-5, and a second oriel window was added.

The Chapel (normally open Tuesday-Friday, 9.00-12.00, 2.00-4.00; Mondays and Saturdays, 9.00-12.00) is in a

⊲ St John's College, Bridge of Sighs

mainly 13th-century style, with a tower 163 feet high and an apse reminiscent of the Sainte-Chapelle's in Paris, On Ascension Day, a service is held at the top of the tower. This would not have been possible if the building had been constructed in accordance with the original design which envisaged a spire at the intersection of the chapel and the ante-chapel, but a former scholar suggested a tower and offered to pay part of the cost. The Chapel contains an interesting monument, removed from the old chapel, to

Hugh Ashton, who died in 1522. It has his recumbent effigy above a second effigy. Ashton's rebus, an ash-leaf growing from a tun, is carved in the stone canopy and is also incorporated in the iron grating. The stained glass depicts scenes from the life of St. John, the predominating colours being red and green.

Above the doorway leading to Second Court is a statue of the Lady Margaret, and over staircase G, on the south side of First Court, is an inscription, STAG NOVR 15, 1777. On that day, members of the college were surprised when horsemen rode into the court in pursuit of a stag which took refuge in the entrance to this staircase. The animal had first been sighted many miles away and had been chased for several hours.

The upper floor to the right of the Gateway was the original Library. St. John's possesses the most handsome of the Gateway-towers and the striking coloured ornamentation towards the street commemorates the Lady Margaret, the daisies and marguerites being an allusion to her name. The curious mythological animals with the head of a goat and the body of an antelope are called yales. The statue of St. John was put up in 1662 to replace an earlier statue removed during the Civil War. The two turrets were rebuilt on a steel frame in 1934-35, when cracks caused by traffic vibration appeared. The small garden opposite was the site of All Saints-in-the-Jewry, demolished in 1865. The outer wall of the tower reached to the edge of the pavement, and pedestrians walked through a passage beneath the tower.

St John's College Chapel

Second Walk

Corpus — Peterhouse — Pembroke — Emmanuel — Christ's

From the Market Square, go along Peas Hill to the west of the Guildhall. The church of St. Edward is more closely associated with the birth of the Reformation in England than any other in the country. Three of the leading exponents of the new doctrines were burned alive, and are commemorated by a tablet in the church: "To the Glory of God and to honour those from this Parish who in the years 1523 to 1525 met near by at the White Horse Inn and there sought out the principles of the English Reformation.

> Thomas Bilney † 1531
> Robert Barnes † 1540
> Hugh Latimer † 1555"

When the church of St. John Zachary was demolished to form part of the site for King's College, Henry VI granted the advowson of St. Edward's to Trinity Hall and it became a Peculiar, outside the jurisdiction of the diocese. For the students of Trinity Hall and Clare who had worshipped in St. John Zachary, two small chapels were added on each side of the chancel.

The earliest part is the base of the tower built in the 13th century, and the nave, originally without aisles, was constructed in about 1400. The pulpit of about 1510, with beautiful linenfold panelling, from which Latimer and other divines preached, is preserved in the church. The night-watchman's chair made in about 1480 came from a church in Dorset; it provides a link with King Edward, the patron saint, who was murdered at Corfe Castle in 978.

A woman who died on 17 August 1650, aged 112, was buried in the churchyard, and in the parish register is an entry:

> Elinor Gaskin said
> She lived four-score years a maid
> And twenty and two years a married wife
> and ten years a widow, and then she left this life.

Turn right into Bene't Street. The Eagle Hotel, a former coaching inn, has a picturesque courtyard. The bedrooms were reached by an exterior staircase.

The Saxon tower of the church of St. Bene't is the oldest building in the county, about 950 years old: it was already standing when William the Conqueror landed.

Thomas Hobson, the famous Cambridge carrier, was buried in the chancel in 1632, and Fabian Stedman, the inventor of change-ringing, was parish clerk here in about 1650. The first organized peal of bells in England was probably rung from this tower.

Go down the passage between the church and the bank to **Corpus Christi College**. The students of the college worshipped in St. Bene't's church until Dr. Cosyn, Master from 1487 to 1515, erected the building between the college and the church, with a chapel on each floor. Corpus is unique among the Cambridge colleges in that it was founded in 1352 by two of the town guilds, the guilds of Corpus Christi and of the Blessed Virgin Mary, in order to train persons fitted to make "supplication to God for the souls of every one of the Fraternity as he departed out of this life".

The Old Court, the first closed quadrangle to be completed in Cambridge, was probably finished by 1378. It has not been greatly altered, and gives a remarkably good impression of the appearance of a medieval college, although the buttresses were added later, garrets were built in the sixteenth century, and many of the windows have been enlarged. In early times, four students occupied each room; the walls were not plastered, there were no ceilings, rushes covered the floor, and there was no heating.

St. Bene't's Church Tower

◁ *Market Place c.1840*

Corpus Christi College Gallery

The Old Hall is now a kitchen, and beyond this is the small former Master's Lodge. A plaque commemorates the dramatists Marlowe and Fletcher, who studied at Corpus.

A passage beside the Old Hall leads into New Court built in 1823-27 to the plans of William Wilkins, who considered it to be his best work in the Gothic style; in accordance with his wishes he was buried in the Chapel. The Hall, on an upper floor, has an open timber roof, linenfold panelling, the Royal Arms behind the dais, and fine armorial glass.

The Library, which may be visited from Mondays to Fridays from 14.00 to 16.00, is on the first floor, opposite the Hall, and contains one of the most important collections of manuscripts and early printed books in the country, assembled by Archbishop Parker after the dissolution of the monasteries, and given to the college. Matthew Parker was admitted to Corpus in 1533, became chaplain to Anne Boleyn, Master of the College in 1544, and Archbishop of Canterbury on the accession of Elizabeth I.

When the Archbishop gave this unique collection to his old college he stipulated that it should be kept under three locks, the keys to be held by the Master and two Fellows; the books and manuscripts were to be inspected annually by the Masters of Gonville and Caius and of Trinity Hall, and should more than a certain number of the books be missing, the collection would be forfeited to Caius.

Leave by the main entrance. **St. Catharine's College** lies across the road. This college was founded in 1473 by Robert Woodlark, Provost of King's College. By 1673 the original buildings were in such a bad condition that most of them were demolished. A Hall and west and south ranges were completed by 1695. The Chapel, begun in 1703 by Robert Grumbold, has a plain ceiling and a fine reredos carved by John Austin. There is an interesting memorial to Mrs. Dawes, the young wife of Sir William Dawes who was Master when the Chapel was built, and who became Vice-Chancellor when only twenty-six years old. She died before her husband left Cambridge to become Bishop of Chester and later Archbishop of York.

In 1757 the Ramsden Building designed by James Essex continued the south range in the style of the earlier work. The college is partly on the site of an inn owned by Hobson, who was born in 1544 and whose six-horse waggons made a weekly journey to London for about sixty years. The phrase 'Hobson's choice, that or none' arose because he kept forty horses for hire and always insisted that the horse that had been rested for the longest time should be taken first. He became one of Cambridge's wealthiest citizens, and in 1628 gave property in St. Andrew's Street for a Spinning House, a workhouse for the poor, and "a house of Correction for unruly and stubborn rogues".

In 1965-8 King's and St. Catharine's carried out a joint scheme for new buildings between the two colleges, designed by Fello Atkinson. These include a new Hall for St. Catharine's. Return to Trumpington Street and turn right, passing the church of St. Botolph. There was a church here in the 12th century; the nave and aisles were rebuilt in the first half of the 14th century, the tower in the 15th. On the other side of the road is the Pitt Building; this and the buildings behind it were formerly the University Printing Press, but there is now a modern works elsewhere. A national fund was raised to commemorate Pitt the Younger; when statues had been erected in Westminster Abbey and Hanover Square, a great deal of money remained, and a bishop suggested that it should be used to enlarge the University Press. The administrators of the fund agreed to pay for this building, which is almost opposite Pembroke College, where Pitt had studied for seven years. It looks somewhat like a church, and hoaxers have sometimes told new students that they must attend church there on their first Sunday in Cambridge.

The church of St. Mary-the-Less, or Little St. Mary's, was built in 1340-52 to replace an earlier church dedicated to St. Peter. The students of Peterhouse used it for their devotions until 1632, and there is a gallery which gave direct access from the college. It has a beautiful east window, and on the wall just inside the entrance is a tablet in memory of the Rev. Godfrey Washington, of the same family as George Washington, who was minister from 1705 until 1729. Above the monument are the arms of the Washington family, with bands and stars from which the flag of the United States was derived.

The open channels on both sides of the street have their origin in a scheme of 1610 to bring water into the town from springs several miles away by constructing the Little New River. Until about 1794 the channel was almost in the centre of the roadway but, after vehicles had fallen into it, the water was diverted to the sides of the street.

Beyond the church is **Peterhouse**, the oldest college in Cambridge. In 1280 Hugh de Balsham, Bishop of Ely, placed some scholars in the Hospital of St. John, but there were conflicts with the brethren, and in 1284 he removed them to two hostels and gave them the tithes of St. Peter's church. When he died two years later, he left money with which the college bought more land and began to erect a Hall. Lack of funds prevented the erection of any other buildings for 130 years.

The Fellows' Building, overlooking the churchyard, was designed in a Palladian style by James Burrough in 1738-42. The corner room on the top floor was occupied by Thomas Gray, the poet. Some of his neighbours were often drunk, and Gray was afraid that they might cause a fire, so he secured a rope ladder. Students kindled a fire below his window one night and shouted 'Fire'. The popular story is that the poet descended in his nightshirt, but it is more probable that he looked out and decided that he was being hoaxed. At all events, he was dissatisfied because the college did not punish the students, and he migrated to Pembroke College across the road.

Peterhouse ▷

The Chapel, flanked by colonnades rebuilt in 1709, was begun in 1628, and is the most interesting Cambridge building of its period, a combination of several styles of architecture. There is a fine timber ceiling, and the east window contains 17th century Flemish glass depicting a scene designed by Rubens. The stained glass in the north and south windows was executed in rich colours by Professor Ainmüller of Munich in 1855-8, who at about the same time designed glass for St. Paul's Cathedral, and they are among the best works of the period. Beneath the east window is a 16th-century German wood carving.

Near the entrance, a stone in the floor inscribed 'W.S. 1857-1958' is in memory of William Stone, who had promised to leave money to the college, but did not die until he was aged 101. With his gift an 8-storey block, one of the best modern buildings in Cambridge, was erected in 1963-4 in the extensive grounds where deer were once kept. The grounds are enclosed towards Coe Fen by a wall built about 400 years ago.

Principal Court was ashlared by Burrough in 1728. The Hall, erected in 1286, was much restored by Sir Giles Gilbert Scott in 1866-8, when the oriel window and the buttresses were added. The wall decorations and the tiles of the fireplace, also the glass of the oriel window, were designed by William Morris.

A Library east of the Hall was built in 1590 with money bequeathed by Andrew Perne, who was Master and five times Vice-Chancellor. He changed his religious beliefs several times, and students invented a new Latin verb, *pernare*, meaning 'to rat, turn, change often'. The Master's Lodge, on the opposite side of Trumpington Street, was built by a Fellow in 1702, and is an attractive example of the domestic architecture of the period.

Pembroke College was founded in 1347 by the Countess of Pembroke, who was descended from Henry III. The original site was only large enough for a court 90 feet by 45 feet, the smallest in the university, which was begun in 1365, but provided for all of the needs of the college for about 250 years. Just inside the gateway, to the left, is the Old Chapel, licensed by the Pope in 1354 and the first of the college chapels. It has a beautiful plaster ceiling of 1690 by Henry Doogood of London, who worked in more than thirty of Wren's churches in the City. The building was later used as a library.

The original Hall and the south range of the court were demolished in 1874-5 by Waterhouse, who then built a new Hall which was lengthened in 1925 by taking in the Combination Room, and chambers were provided in the upper part. To the right is the Chapel built in 1663-4, the first completed work of Sir Christopher Wren, also the earliest sacred building in England in a pure classical style. His uncle, Dr. Matthew Wren, Bishop of Ely at the time of the Civil War, was imprisoned in the Tower of London for

Aerial photograph of Cambridge ▷
(courtesy of Cambridge Evening News)

eighteen years, and vowed that when he should regain his liberty he would do something to thank the Almighty. He had been a Fellow of Pembroke, and he asked his nephew to design the chapel. It was slightly lengthened by Sir George Gilbert Scott to provide a short chancel separated from the original plain rectangle by Corinthian marble columns. There is a fine plaster ceiling, a painting by Federico Barocci (1526-1612) which once belonged to Sir Joshua Reynolds, and 17th century cushions which came from Ely Cathedral.

Ivy Court has two 17th century ranges, beyond which are a range by Waterhouse and New Building, designed by the younger G.G. Scott in 1883, and one of the best of its period. Waterhouse designed the red brick range beyond the Chapel, and the Library. Near the latter is a statue of William Pitt, facing the rooms that he occupied until he entered Parliament in 1781, and became Prime Minister two years later, when he was only twenty-five. Pembroke is also the college of the poets Edmund Spenser, Thomas Gray and Christopher Smart.

Roger Long, Master from 1733 to 1770, who was Professor of Astronomy and interested in mechanical devices, built the first planetarium, in which thirty persons could sit. When a handle was turned, the audience could see "the relative situation and successive motions of the heavenly bodies". He also invented a boat which he propelled by moving his feet, which appears to have been the forerunner of the similar boats to be found at the seaside.

Leave the college by the gateway in Pembroke Street, which soon becomes Downing Street, with university buildings on both sides. The entrance to **Emmanuel College** is opposite the end of this street. The college occupies the site of a Dominican Friary. The extensive grounds and some good buildings were purchased by Sir Walter Mildmay, Chancellor of the Exchequer to Elizabeth I, in 1583.

The chapel of the friars was converted into a Hall, and the refectory was repaired to become the Chapel, although it ran from north to south. A long range with short wings was built to face St. Andrew's Street, and another building was put up on the south side of the present Front Court. Early in the 17th century the college was the principal centre of Puritanism in Cambridge.

The main façade towards the street was rebuilt by Essex and completed in 1775. The Hall, on the left side of the court, was ashlar-faced and redecorated in 1764 by Essex, who constructed the delicate stucco ceiling. The Westmoreland Building across the court replaced an earlier building in 1719-22. Before you visit the Chapel, go through a passage to the left into New Court, which in spite of its name was the first court of the college. Here stood the Friars' refectory which the founder converted into a chapel. It later became a library. The screen of the old chapel was discovered behind plaster on the south wall during alterations made in 1932-3.

◁ *Pembroke College*

Return to Front Court to see the Chapel with its flanking colonnades, designed by Wren in 1666. A tablet near the entrance commemorates John Harvard, who entered Emmanuel in 1627. He bequeathed half of his fortune and his library to found Harvard College in the U.S.A. Many other Puritan scholars of the college sought freedom across the Atlantic. The beautiful plaster ceiling is decorated with flowers, fruit and leaves; the 17th century woodwork was executed by Cornelius Austin. The oak communion rails are of the late 17th century, while the cut-glass chandelier was presented to the college in 1732. The painting, *The Return of the Prodigal Son*, by Jacopo Amigoni (1675-1752), was given two years later.

The lake in the attractive garden was once the fishpond of the Friars. Brick Building, at right angles to the east of Front Court, was built in 1633-4, and has been restored but not greatly altered. There are also 19th century buildings, and some good recent ranges towards the south. North Court, built in 1910-14, lies on the opposite side of Emmanuel Street, and is connected with the rest of the college by an underground tunnel.

Christ's College is also in St. Andrew's Street. The college of Godshouse, which had moved here from Milne Street, remained small until, in 1505, Lady Margaret Beaufort provided additional buildings and endowments to

◁ *Emmanuel College Chapel*   *Christ's College* ▷

support sixty members. She changed the name to Christ's and arranged for the construction of the Hall, Master's Lodge, and other buildings to complete the First Court, which is one of the most attractive in Cambridge. She reserved the first floor and the attics of the Lodge for herself, and sometimes resided there.

The street frontage was ashlar-faced in the 18th century and extended in 1895-7. The Gateway of 1505-11 has Lady Margaret's coat of arms above the arch, and the doors are original. The Chapel is on the left side of the court. The timber roof is original; the notable panelling was made by John Austin in 1702-3. The east window depicts the Lady Margaret and Bishop Fisher in one corner, Henry VII in the other, also a view of the college, and Christ above on a cloud.

The north windows have coloured glass of the late 15th and early 16th centuries. High in the wall to the right is a small window through which the Lady Margaret could look into the chapel from one of her rooms in the Lodge. The large brass eagle lectern, resembling one in St. Mark's Venice, is one of the finest Pre-Reformation lecterns in England. Near the organ is a remarkable monument to Sir Thomas Baines and Sir John Finch, made by Joseph Catterns in 1684. Although Baines was poor and Finch rich, they formed a friendship in their student days and remained inseparable throughout their lives. Finch studied medicine in Padua, became a professor in Pisa, and later a diplomat in Constantinople, where Baines was doctor to the embassy.

When Baines died, Finch had his body embalmed and sent it to be buried in Christ's College. Finch died a few months later, and was buried beside his friend. The Hall was rebuilt, using the old materials, in 1875, when the walls were made six feet higher and an oriel was constructed. There are portraits of John Milton, William Paley, Charles Darwin and the foundress.

Fellows' Building, in Second Court, was erected in 1640-3 and is one of the most interesting of its period. The unknown designer introduced two features then new to Cambridge: upright windows with a mullion and transom cross, and attic windows with alternate triangular and segmental pediments. The doorway in the centre of the building gives access to the beautiful Fellows' Garden, where there is a rectangular bathing-pool with a small 18th century summerhouse and three stone busts, one of John Milton, and a draped urn, on tapering pedestals. The poet, who was at Christ's from 1625 to 1632, had a room on the left side of First Court as it is entered from the street, on the first floor of the first staircase. It is said that a mulberry tree in the garden was planted by him, but the tree is probably the last of 300 planted by the college in the year of Milton's birth.

Beyond Fellows' Building is a third court which includes two ranges designed by Sir Albert Richardson and Eric Haufe in 1948-50 and 1952-3; towards King Street is the first phase of a range designed by Denys Lasdun, with tiers of stepped-back rooms.

Third Walk

Caius — Sidney — Jesus — Magdalene

The church of Great St. Mary's is the University Church and also a parish church. In early times, when the university did not possess a large hall, the nave was used for ceremonies and examinations, and the university paid most of the cost when it was rebuilt between 1478 and 1519. It was still roofless when Henry VII, who visited Cambridge in 1505, presented 100 oak trees from Chesterford Park to cover the nave. The tower, begun in 1491, was not finished until about 80 years later; from its summit there are extensive views over the city.

Great St. Mary's is one of the finest churches of East Anglia in the Later Perpendicular style, and the interior has very tall and slender shafts dividing the nave and aisles into five bays. The galleries were added in 1735 to accommodate the people who went to listen to the University Sermons, while a huge structure called The Throne was built across the chancel for the Vice-Chancellor, Doctors and the University Officers. There was also a very tall pulpit in the centre of the nave. These fittings were taken down in 1863. The famous quarter-hour chimes of the clock were composed in 1793 by the Rev. Joseph Jowett, a Fellow of Trinity Hall, and William Crotch, a very precocious musician. The chimes were copied later for the Stock Exchange, in 1859 for Big Ben at the Houses of Parliament, and later for many clocks throughout the English-speaking world. They are often called the Westminster Quarters, which is unfair to Cambridge, where they originated.

The Senate House, designed by James Gibbs and built in 1722-30, is one of the finest Classical buildings in Cambridge. It is here that leading members of the university meet to discuss new projects and regulations. Degree ceremonies are also held here, including a special assembly in June, when Honorary Degrees are awarded to distinguished persons, English and foreign.

Beside the Senate House is the east front of the Old Schools built in 1754-8 to plans made by Burrough, though Stephen Wright designed the elevations and supervised the construction. This building was formerly a part of the University Library until the new library was built in 1934.

Great St. Mary's Church

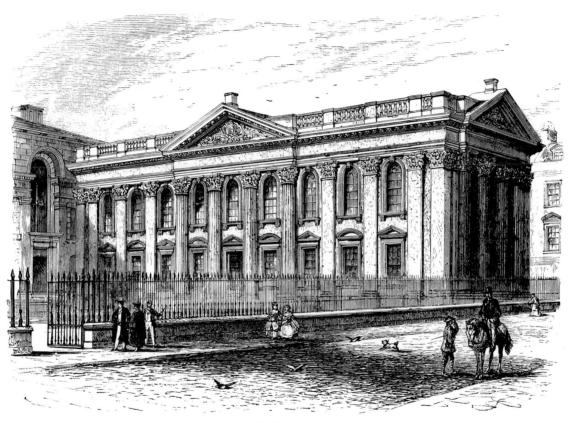

The Senate House

In the centre of the lawn is a bronze replica of the Warwick vase. The original marble vase, now at Warwick Castle, was found at the bottom of a lake at Hadrian's villa near Rome.

The bookshop at the corner of Trinity Street is the oldest continuously used in England; books have been sold here since 1581. To the left of the street is the range designed by Alfred Waterhouse in 1870 for Caius College.

Go down Senate House Passage, where, on the left beyond the Senate House, is Cockerell's Neo-Classical building of 1836-42 which was erected to extend the University Library. It is now the Squire Law Library. Enter **Gonville and Caius College** through the distinctive Gate of Honour or, if it is closed, through the gate in Trinity Street.

Edmund Gonville, a priest and the son of a Frenchman domiciled in England, founded Gonville Hall in 1347 on a site near Corpus, but the college soon moved to part of its present site. In 1557 Dr. John Caius (pronounced 'keys') decided to refound and enlarge "that pore house now called Gonville Hall". He had studied there, and then went to Padua to study medicine and became a professor, later returning to England, where he was appointed physician to Edward VI and Mary.

He gave his old college money and books, but it was not well administered, and he was persuaded to become the Master in 1559. In France and Italy he had become familiar with Renaissance architecture, and he began to design noble new buildings for his college. The Gate of Virtue, to the right, is one of the earliest buildings in the country in the

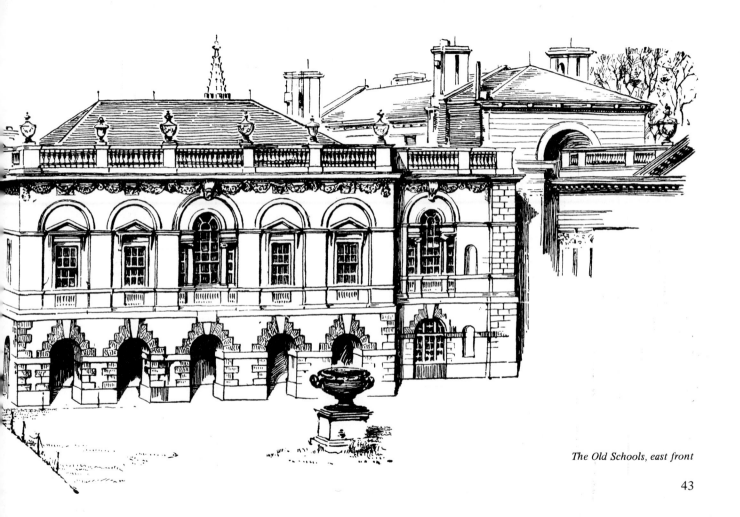

The Old Schools, east front

Renaissance style. He decided that his court would have buildings on only three sides "lest the air, from being confined within a narrow space, should become foul", the fourth side being closed by a wall and the ornate gateway constructed in 1575 after the death of Caius, but to his designs, probably inspired by a Roman tomb. The stone was originally painted white, with some parts coloured and gilded.

The college was formerly entered through another gate, the Gate of Humility. Caius had a love of symbolism, and his three gateways symbolised the years of residence of a student, who would enter through the Gate of Humility, often pass through the Gate of Virtue, and finally leave by the Gate of Honour to receive his degree.

The Chapel was built in about 1393, lengthened in 1637 and considerably altered in 1716-26. There is a striking monument to Dr. Caius, and another commemorates Dr. Perse who died in 1615 and left money to found the Cambridge grammar school for boys that (like the later girls' school) bears his name.

The small Gonville Court beyond the Chapel was the first to be built, but 140 years elapsed before it was completed. It was refaced by Burrough in 1753. To the left is the entrance to the Hall, open 10.00-12.00, 2.30-6.00, which is on the first floor; it was built by Salvin in 1853 and repaired in recent years. There are portraits of William Harvey, who discovered the circulation of the blood; Thomas Gresham, who founded the Royal Exchange; and

Caius College, Gate of Virtue

44

Jeremy Taylor, the son of a Cambridge barber who became a bishop. On the wall near the High Table is a small flag of the college which Dr. Wilson, a member of Captain Scott's expedition in 1912, flew at the South Pole. St. Michael's Court was erected on the other side of Trinity Street in 1903.

St. Michael's Church in Trinity Street was rebuilt by Hervey de Stanton after he had founded Michaelhouse in 1323; he is buried in the large chancel which he built for his student-priests, the nave being for the use of the parishioners. The church became redundant, and the nave has been partitioned off to form a meeting-hall.

Continue along Trinity Street to just beyond the post office, where there is an entrance to the 19th century Whewell's Court, a detached part of Trinity. To the right of this court is the important modern Wolfson Building which few Cambridge people have ever seen, because it is not visible from the street. This development provided large shops for Heffer and for Sainsbury on the ground floor; on a podium above them is a 5-storey block containing 90 student study-bedrooms. Seen from above, the shape of the building resembles a liner in dry dock.

Continue through Whewell's Court to Sidney Street and turn to the right to visit **Sidney Sussex College** across the road. In 1594 the executors of Frances Sidney, Countess of Sussex, obtained a lease of the ground that had belonged to the Franciscans and founded a college for a Master, 10 Fellows and 20 Scholars. Most of the monastic buildings had been destroyed, but the refectory was divided into two floors to serve as the Chapel with a Library above.

The entrance lodge was built by Wyatville who, in 1821-32, faced the buildings of both courts with cement and introduced gables and battlements to give a Tudor-Gothic appearance. His alterations created a uniform E-plan design out of the existing dissimilar courts. Hall Court, to the left, is in main the building erected by Ralph Symons in 1595-8; here is the Hall, with panelled walls and a plaster ceiling with stucco ornament, and a large semicircular bay window. There is a famous portrait of Oliver Cromwell, who entered the college in 1616.

The range north-east of Hall Court was built in 1890, and the beautiful grounds were first laid out in the 18th century. The Chapel is in the Second Court. It was designed by Essex in 1776-82 and rebuilt and lengthened by T.H. Lyon in 1912, with a barrel-vaulted plaster ceiling and marble paving. The oak panelling and fittings are very elaborate and unusual. The large painting by Giovanni Battista Pittoni (1687-1767) was purchased in 1783 for twenty guineas. The east side of the court is formed by Sir Francis Clerke's range of 1628, though much altered. A range facing Sussex Street with student rooms above the shops was designed by E. R. Barrow and erected in 1938-9; there are also 20th-century blocks towards King Street.

After the Restoration, the body of Oliver Cromwell was exhumed and beheaded, and the head remained impaled on a stave on Westminster Hall for twenty-five years until it

Sidney Sussex College

was blown down in a gale. The head eventually came into the possession of a lady who some years ago bequeathed it to Sidney Sussex College; it was buried near the Chapel by the Master and two Fellows on 25 March 1960.

Leave the college and turn to the right, then right again into Jesus Lane, where you will soon come to the Ionic portico of the Pitt Club, a building erected in 1863 as a swimming-bath by the Roman Bath Co. Ltd. It was not a commercial success, and the building was adapted for the use of the Pitt Club, a university club originally founded to honour the memory of Pitt the Younger. On the corner of Park Street is 'Little Trinity', an attractive 3-storey early 18th-century building, and in the wall across the road, the old gateway of Sidney College which was moved when the new entrance lodge was constructed.

It is probable that no more than one in a hundred of the people who are familiar with the colleges near the river go to see **Jesus College** yet it is one of the most interesting, with survivals from the Nunnery of Saint Radegund. In 1496 John Alcock, Bishop of Ely, visited the nunnery and found ruinous buildings occupied by only two women. He obtained a licence from Henry VII to suppress the nunnery and to establish a college. For the first time in Cambridge, a suppressed religious house became the site for a college.

The college is entered through a gate in Jesus Lane built by Robert Grumbold in 1703, and a path between two ancient walls which is known as "the chimney". Bishop Alcock arranged for the construction of the Gatehouse in 1497. It was originally more impressive because the buildings beside it were of two storeys; a third storey was added in 1718. The Bishop's rebus, a cock standing on a globe, can be seen on the Gatehouse and elsewhere in the college. The range ahead, beyond the gate, was put up in 1638-40. To the right, all of the buildings in Cloister Court formed part of the nunnery, although Alcock increased their height to three storeys and inserted the fine timber ceilings in the cloisters. The brick arches were constructed by Essex.

For a college originally intended to possess only a Master, six Fellows and a few Scholars, the church of the nuns was much too large. The aisles of the nave and of the chancel were demolished, and the western part of the nave was converted into chambers, later to become the Master's Lodge. Five lancets in the east wall were replaced by a large Perpendicular window. The Chapter House was also demolished, with the exception of the west wall, in which the doorway and windows were blocked up, but this beautiful early work of about 1230 has been visible again since 1893, when the plaster which had concealed it was removed.

The present Chapel consists of the antechapel, formerly the eastern part of the conventual nave, the transepts and the choir. On the west wall is a striking white marble monument to Tobias Rustat, Yeoman of the Robes to Charles II, who died in 1695. The north transept is the

oldest part, and was probably built in about 1160, the nave in about 1200. Pugin reconstructed the east end of the magnificent thirteenth century chancel in 1849-53; he put in five lancet windows based on surviving fragments of the original work, also the screen, stalls, altar, and the tiles in the crossing and the choir.

Further repairs were carried out in 1864-7, when Bodley strengthened and refaced the tower, and new ceilings were designed by William Morris. A little later, most of the windows were reglazed, most of them to designs by Burne-Jones.

The kitchens of the nunnery were on the ground floor with a refectory above them. Bishop Alcock heightened the walls and refaced them with brick, inserted new windows and a new roof. The Hall has a very beautiful 3-sided oriel window, the armorial stained glass being by Morris. The panelling of the screen and the dais was executed in 1703. The Hall was lengthened by Waterhouse in 1875, and the gallery was added in 1962, when the oriel which had been in the west wall was rebuilt in the farther wall. The Upper Hall has an early sixteenth century open-timbered roof.

Unfortunately, the beautiful Old Library dating from the foundation of the college is not normally open to visitors. There are several modern ranges, including Chapel Court designed by P. Morley Horder in 1930. The coat of

◁ Jesus College, entrance gateway

arms, supported by angels, over one of the arches, was carved by Eric Gill. The grounds of the College are more spacious than any others in the University, and North Court, designed by D.W. Roberts and completed in 1965, stands apart from the remainder of the college. Former members of Jesus include Thomas Cranmer, who lost his Fellowship when he married the niece of the landlady of the Dolphin Inn, but regained it after his wife died in childbirth; Laurence Sterne, the author of *Tristram Shandy*; and the poet Samuel Taylor Coleridge.

Leave Jesus College and return down Jesus Lane, then turn to the right into Bridge Street. Beyond the shops, and lying back from the road, are the premises of the Union Society, the famous debating society of the University, and one of the few academic buildings damaged by bombing during the last war.

We next come to one of the most interesting buildings in Cambridge, the Church of the Holy Sepulchre, more usually called the Round Church, one of the four round churches in England. Between 1114 and 1130, members of the fraternity of the Holy Sepulchre were granted a site for the church, and the circular nave and ambulatory, also a small chancel, were built during the first half of the 12th century. A north chapel was added later, and in the 15th century a polygonal belfry was placed above the nave. In 1841 the church was thoroughly restored by the Cambridge Camden Society. The belfry gave way to a stone vault over the circular nave, and windows were altered to recreate the

12th century style. The chancel walls were rebuilt and a south aisle and bell-turret were added.

Beyond the Round Church is an attractive group of old buildings which have recently been restored. Until just before the Second World War there were houses and shops along the opposite side of the street, until they were demolished for extensions to St. John's College.

Magdalene Bridge, formerly called the Great Bridge, is a place of considerable historical importance. In early times, there was first a ford, and later a succession of wooden bridges, the first coming into existence between 731 and 875. In 1279, Commissioners of Edward I found that the bridge was "so broken and dislocated that the carriages of noble persons and others fell into the water in such a way that both men and horses come to the surface with difficulty". Townswomen convicted of being common scolds were placed in a ducking chair which hung from a pulley fastened to a beam near the middle of the bridge, and were immersed three times in the water.

Almost everything needed by the townsfolk came by lighter or barge from Lynn: Quayside was one of the places where goods were landed. It formerly extended for about 150 feet, with quays and warehouses on both banks of the river and on both sides of the bridge. Salmon's Lane separated Magdalene College and a number of houses, those beside the river being mostly alehouses used by the bargees. One of the commodities unloaded here was sedge, a coarse reed used for lighting fires. Every college had a sedge loft, and the bedmakers wore sedge-gloves to protect their hands from the sharp edges of the sedge. From the bridge one can see on a gable of Magdalene College, formerly called Buckingham College, a stone carving of a chained swan. The coat of arms of the Duke of Buckingham was supported by two chained swans.

The main buildings of **Magdalene College** are to the right, just over the bridge. Four monasteries built small hostels for monks studying in Cambridge, and later the Duke of Buckingham constructed a Hall for them, and the college was first called Buckingham College. After the dissolution of the monasteries, Thomas Lord Audley was granted a licence, in 1542, to found the college of St. Mary Magdalene for a Master and eight Fellows. The range facing the street does not look ancient because it has been restored, but the whole of the court was built from about 1430 to 1580, the Renaissance gateway in 1585. The buildings on the right side of the court bear, above the doorways, the arms of the monasteries which supported the original hostels. On the left are the Library and the Chapel, which latter, though restored and lengthened, is in part the Chapel of Buckingham College. The small Hall of 1519 has also been altered, but the windows are original. A beautiful double staircase of 1714 leads to the Gallery and Combination Room, and the arms of Queen Anne occupy the whole of the wall above the panelling behind the High Table. The portraits include those of Charles Kingsley, Samuel Pepys, A.C. Benson and T.S. Eliot.

The Round Church

The fine Pepys Building is in the Second Court. The diarist gave money towards its construction and the inscription *Biblioteca Pepysiana,* 1724 with his arms in the pediment of the central window were put up when his library of 3,000 volumes arrived. The books are kept in the original cases of red oak; the smaller books stand on little pedestals shaped like the spine of a book, so that the tops of all the books are on the same level. The manuscripts of the famous diary are also preserved here. The library is normally open to visitors on weekdays during the terms, 14.30-15.30.

The most recent additions to the college lie on the other side of Magdalene Street, behind what is the largest group of medieval domestic buildings still existing in the city. When the red brick range of 1931-2 was designed by Sir Edwin Lutyens, two other ranges were planned, and all of the old buildings would have been demolished. Fortunately, they were reprieved, and most have been adapted for student use by David Roberts, who also designed a handsome 3-storey building in yellow brick and a 4-storey block beside the river, as well as Buckingham Court, built in 1968-9. Among the buildings facing the street, mostly timber-framed and plastered, and erected from medieval times to the 18th century, the most picturesque is the former Cross Keys Inn, now occupied by the Magdalene Street Gallery. The part of this building at right angles to the street is of the early 16th century.

Magdalene College, First Court

◁ *Magdalene College, Pepys Library*

Newnham College

Fourth Walk

Newnham — Churchill — Fitzwilliam — New Hall

This walk enables the visitor to see some of the recent university and college buildings, including the University Library, the Arts Faculties buildings in Sidgwick Avenue, and three post-war colleges.

On the far side of Silver Street Bridge is **Darwin**, the first college for graduates, which was established jointly by Caius, St. John's and Trinity in 1965 in three existing Victorian houses, *The Old Granary* and *Newnham Grange*, which had belonged to the Darwin family, and *The Hermitage*. The two latter were linked in 1966-8 by a building that enhances their appearance, and an octagonal dining hall on stilts was erected towards Newnham Terrace.

Continue straight ahead into Sidgwick Avenue, where Newnham College is on the left, beyond Ridley Hall. **Newnham**, the second college for women, began in 1871 when five students occupied a house in Regent Street. After a brief sojourn in Merton Hall, adjoining the School of Pythagoras, the first college buildings were opened in 1875. Most were designed by Basil Champneys in a red-brick Dutch style. Recent additions include an extension to the Library and the Y-shaped New Building designed by Lyster and Grillet.

On the other side of Sidgwick Avenue is an important group of university buildings for the Faculties of English, Economics and Politics, History, Modern Languages, Moral Sciences and Oriental Studies. Most were designed by Sir Hugh Casson and Neville Conder, and construction began in 1956. There is a tall block of ten lecture theatres seating a total of 950 people, and two halls, Lady Mitchell Hall seating 450, and Little Hall seating 150.

James Stirling's History Faculty building (1964-8) is one of the most original and striking in Cambridge. Two wings of an L-shaped faculty block enclose a tent-shaped glazed roof over the library which can accommodate 350 readers.

In West Road to the left, is the first phase of the new Music School, with a Concert Hall. Now turn to the right to visit Harvey Court belonging to Caius College, designed by Sir Leslie Martin and Colin St. John Wilson and erected in 1960-2. It should be viewed from the south, open side, where a wide and imposing series of steps leads up to three stepped tiers of rooms on terraces, with a breakfast room beneath the centre.

At the end of West Road turn left into Queen's Road and go through Memorial Court of Clare College, designed by Sir Giles Gilbert Scott, built in 1924-35 and extended in 1955. Beyond Memorial Court is the large new **University Library** of 1931-4 by the same architect, a steel-framed building of russet brick, 420 feet long and with a massive central tower 160 feet high.

The University Library is the third largest in the country, with nearly four million books. When it was built, it was thought that the forty-five miles of shelving would suffice for about fifty years, but the Library has already been considerably enlarged. There are guided tours through the richly decorated interior at 3.00p.m.

In Burrell's Walk turn left towards Grange Road. Here are recent buildings erected by Trinity College, and across the road, the site upon which Robinson College is being built. Turn right, then left into Madingley Road, where you will soon come to **Churchill College**, founded as a national monument to Sir Winston Spencer Churchill. Construction began in 1961, and Richard Sheppard designed a number of connecting courts of 3-storey brick and concrete buildings for the first phase. The Hall on an upper floor is reached by a staircase off the main entrance corridor. It can seat 300 persons, is 50 feet high, and has a triple-barrel vaulted roof covered externally with copper. Two walls are covered with wood panelling of a bold ribbed design. Below the Hall is a snack bar.

The free-standing Library group contains the Bracken Library with a Jean Lurçat tapestry presented by Charles de Gaulle. The Bevin reading-room for post-graduates is on an upper floor, and the Wolfson Hall seats 250. A recent addition is a building to contain the Winston Churchill archives. After much controversy, a small Chapel was built away from the main buildings and near blocks of flats for research students and married graduates. In the extensive grounds are sculptures by Henry Moore and Barbara Hepworth.

Also in Storey's Way, just around the first bend, is an entrance to **Fitzwilliam College**. In 1869, a small number of men who did not belong to a college were allowed to study in the university. They were under the control of a Censor, and Fitzwilliam House in Trumpington Street became a meeting-place for them. After the university had decided that Fitzwilliam should be accorded full collegiate status, the construction of buildings designed by Denys Lasdun began in 1961. The Hall and the Library were placed near the centre of the site, with residential ranges around them. The upper part of the Hall has a striking silhouette of concrete arches with spreading soffits, glazed all round. The Library is above two Common Rooms, and there is a room seating 210 for lectures, music or drama.

Leave by the entrance in Huntingdon Road. **New Hall** is on an adjoining site to the right. This, the third college for women, was founded in 1954, but for the first ten years occupied The Hermitage in Silver Street. The present site was given by the Darwin family, and building in a white brick began in 1962. The architects, Chamberlin, Powell and Bon, designed a 3-sided court with wide cloisters and a sunken pool. The Hall is surmounted by a large dome of eight separate leaves; the Library is placed to the west of the court.

Other College and University Buildings

Selwyn College, at first classed as a 'public hostel' and not as an 'approved foundation' until 1926, was opened in 1882 for Church of England men of moderate means. Sir A.W. Blomfield designed two ranges, one towards the street and another to the north of the court, including the Chapel, in a modern Tudor style. A Jacobean style was adopted for the south range of 1908-9 and the Hall, which has panelling of 1708 from the Anglican Church at Rotterdam. The most recent additions to the college lie on the other side of Grange Road.

Girton College. In the latter part of the 19th century there was a demand for better educational facilities for women, and Emily Davies began to raise money to establish a college. A house at Hitchin was rented in 1869, but by 1872 this was too small and the lease was about to run out. Though Emily Davies at first opposed them members of the committee wished to build at Cambridge, and eventually it was decided to establish the college at Girton, about two miles from the town. One wing and a small Hall, designed by Alfred Waterhouse, were built in 1873 for the first twenty-one students, and later Waterhouse and his son added more buildings in a Tudor style. The college has erected its most recent buildings in Clarkson Road, nearer to the centre of the city.

Downing College. Sir George Downing, who died in 1749, left money for a new college, but legal difficulties caused delays and his college was not founded until 1807. A very large site was secured, and William Wilkins won a competition

Selwyn College

to design the buildings, for which he chose a neo-Grecian style, placing them round a spacious lawn. Construction proceeded slowly, and his plans have been modified by later architects.

By 1821 only the east and west ranges, each of four blocks, had been built. Edward Barry completed an unfinished block in 1873 and remodelled the Hall; in 1930-1 Sir Herbert Baker added two L-shaped ranges to the north. The central range, including an apsed Chapel, was erected by A.T. Scott in 1951-3, and there are also some more recent buildings.

Girton College

Graduate Colleges

In recent years there has been a marked increase in the number of graduates who come to Cambridge from other English and from foreign universities to do research or to obtain a higher degree. The existing colleges could not accommodate them, so a number of colleges exclusively for them have been founded.

American benefactors assisted Clare College to build **Clare Hall** in Herschel Road in 1966-9; Ralph Erskine designed an interesting group of communal rooms, flats and houses, on a site overlooking the University Rugby Ground. **Wolfson College** was originally founded as University College in 1963, and when the first students arrived in 1966 they occupied Bredon House, between Selwyn Gardens and Barton Road. Funds provided by the Wolfson Foundation enabled additional buildings, opened by the Queen in 1977, to be erected. The floor of the entrance hall consists of thin sections of large blocks of granite which came from parts of the old London Bridge which were not sent with the main structure to Arizona. Wolfson provides a collegiate society for some of the teaching, research and administrative staff of the university and for graduates pursuing courses of research for second degrees and diplomas. The 266 students of 1977 came from 41 different countries.

◁ *Downing College*

Lucy Cavendish College, at first housed in Northampton Street, has taken over a large house in Lady Margaret Road.

Corpus College made provision for research students and bachelor Fellows at Leckhampton House in Grange Road by erecting new buildings designed by Philip Dowson of Arup Associates in 1963-4. These two blocks, with pre-cast concrete 'hanging frames' and large windows, are among the most attractive of the post-war buildings.

Other Buildings

University Centre, in Granta Place, off Mill Lane, was erected in 1964-7 to provide a social centre for men and women who could not be attached to the older colleges. This 4-storey building provides catering and recreational facilities and rooms for functions and conferences. Membership is available primarily to senior staff of the university, postgraduate students and visiting scholars, also to the wives or husbands of members.

The **Fitzwilliam Museum** in Trumpington Street is one of the most important in England. The seventh Viscount Fitzwilliam left money and his collection of pictures, engravings, illuminated manuscripts and books to the university, including paintings by Titian, Rembrandt and Veronese. Other benefactors have given many pictures of the Dutch and Flemish schools, early Italian paintings, and works by Constable, Gainsborough, Turner, Augustus John, and Stanley Spencer, among others. There are also many works by French Impressionists. The museum has a large collection of pottery and porcelain, the third most important collection in the world of ancient Greek coins, antiquities from Greece, Rome and Egypt, also armour and weapons.

The imposing Neo-Classical building in the Corinthian order, designed by George Basevi, was begun in 1837. When he died in 1845, after falling through some scaffolding in Ely Cathedral, it was carried on until 1847 by C.R. Cockerell. Lack of funds caused work to be suspended until the main building was completed by E. M. Barry in 1870-5. Considerable extensions have been made in the present century.

The **University Botanic Garden**, with entrances in Trumpington Road, Bateman Street and Hills Road, is primarily intended for teaching and research, but the attractive grounds, including a pond with ducks and moorhens, attract many visitors. The Garden is open daily from 8.00 a.m. until dusk, the greenhouses only in the afternoons.

The early **Scientific Laboratories** of the university were

Fitzwilliam Museum

erected in and around Downing Street, firstly on the site vacated by the Botanic Garden, then on a large site to the south which had originally belonged to Downing College.

The world-famous **Cavendish Laboratory** is in Free School Lane, but a large additional laboratory costing £2.25 million has recently been built in Madingley Road on an extensive site on which it is planned to erect other scientific laboratories. The **Engineering Laboratory** moved to Fen Causeway in 1948 and has since been extended. A new **Chemical Laboratory** was built in Lensfield Road in 1953-60.

CAMBRIDGE MUSEUMS

The principal museums in Cambridge are:

FITZWILLIAM MUSEUM, Trumpington Street.

FOLK MUSEUM, at the corner of Northampton Street and Castle Street (past Magdalene Bridge).

ARCHAEOLOGY AND ETHNOLOGY MUSEUM, Downing Street.

Other museums include:

Kettle's Yard Art Gallery, Northampton Street.

Museum of Classical Archaeology, Little St. Mary's Lane.

Museum of Technology, Cheddars Lane. (Open only on the first Sunday afternoon of the month).

Scott Polar Research Institute, Lensfield Road.

Sedgwick Museum of Geology, Downing Street.

Whipple Museum of the History of Science, Free School Lane.

Zoological Museum, Downing Street.

For current opening times enquire at the Cambridge Tourist Information Centre (behind the Guildhall), Wheeler Street, Tel. 0223 58977 or 0223 53363 after 5.30 p.m. (4.30 p.m. on Fridays) and weekends.